THE BOOK OF WHALES, DOLPHINS, AND PORPOISES

by
Lionel Bender

Illustrated by
Chris Forsey

SMITHMARK

CONTENTS

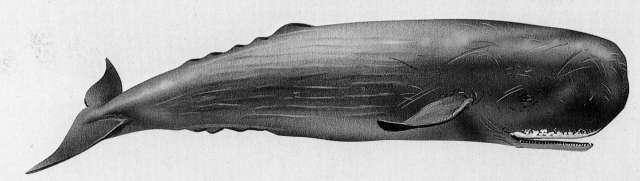

Toothed whale

TOOTHED WHALES

Whales are mammals, just like cats, dogs, monkeys, and people. Mammals are warm-blooded and they breathe in air through their lungs. The female gives birth to live young which she feeds on her milk. Unlike other mammals, whales spend all their lives in water and do not have a coat of hair for warmth.

There are two main types of whales: toothed whales and baleen or whalebone whales. Toothed whales have from two to 200 teeth, which they use to catch and eat fish, squid, and shellfish. They range from small dolphins and porpoises to the giant sperm whale. Baleen whales do not have teeth. Instead they have horny (whalebone) plates which hang from the roof of the mouth. They use these plates to sieve small animals and plants from the water. The largest animal in the world, the blue whale, belongs to this group.

In the first part of The **Book of Whales, Dolphins, and Porpoises** you will find out about the most important toothed whales and in the second part about the baleen whales. Today, whales are in danger of dying out as a result of hunting and pollution of the seas. Many countries have now banned whaling.

Porpoise

Baleen whale

Dolphin

BELUGA
(Delphinapterus leucas)

There are 66 species of toothed whale. All of them have teeth and many use echolocation to find their prey of fish and squid.

Adult beluga, or white, whales (*Delphinapterus leucas*) have creamy white skins. This, and the lack of a fin along the back, are their most noticeable features. At birth, belugas are gray. During their second and third years they change to deep marble-blue and gradually to white.

Belugas live mainly in shallow waters in groups of up to 20. They swim slowly and gracefully at the surface, and feed at all depths. The young feed on shrimps, crabs, and worms. The adults feed on crabs and fish such as cod, halibut, and char. They do not chew their food but swallow it whole.

Whalers used to call the beluga the "sea canary" because of the bird-like calls it uses when swimming at the surface. Underwater, it makes a series of growls and roars which it uses to communicate with other beluga whales.

Motherly love and care
A female beluga nurses her young for up to 8 months. She squeezes her milk glands to squirt milk into the youngster's mouth. Belugas grow up to 20 feet (6 meters) in length and up to 1.5 tons.

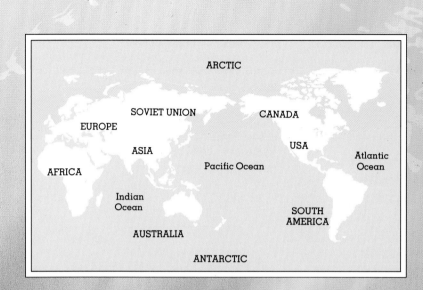

Swimming upriver
Groups of belugas are often seen around estuaries along the Arctic coasts. Some spend all their lives in large seaways such as the St. Lawrence River in Canada. Here, many of them are poisoned by wastes dumped in the river.

Echolocation – sensing with sounds
Belugas use echolocation to find food and air holes in the pack ice among which they live. They do this by sending out high-pitched whistling sounds from the tops of their heads. They can then judge the distance of an object by the time it takes for the echoes of these sounds to return.

7

THE NARWHAL
(Monodon monoceros)

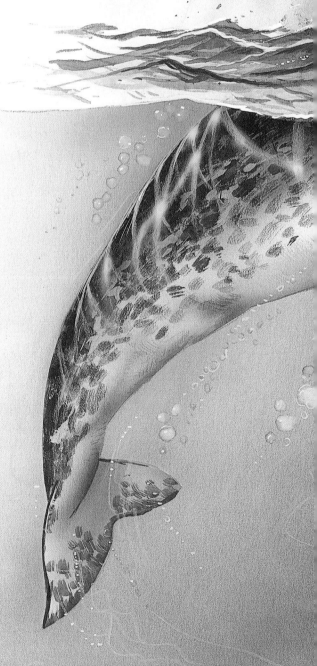

The male narwhal has a spirally twisted tusk up to 10 feet (3 meters) long. This has led some people to call the species the unicorn whale. The tusk is a long canine tooth. Some males develop a pair of tusks; females rarely have them. The exact use of the narwhal's tusk is unknown. It may be used to dig for food on the sea bed, to break a way through thin ice to make a breathing hole, or as a weapon.

Narwhals feed on cuttlefish, squid, shrimps, and fish. Like their close relative the beluga, they swallow their food whole. They suck in their prey as they have no teeth other than their tusks. Narwhals swim quickly and every 40 seconds or so they break out of the water probably to take a short breath. When breathing deeply, they toss their heads sharply up above the surface.

Patchy distribution
Often found alongside belugas, narwhals live in Arctic seas, but mainly in deep water. In the past, male narwhals were hunted for the ivory of their tusks and the species almost died out. As a result, today narwhals are found only in isolated parts of their former range.

Fighting over females
Narwhals are 13–16 feet (4–5 meters) long and can weigh up to 1.5 tons. Male narwhals use their tusks in jousting contests. The winner will mate with a female. The battles are more tests of strength than fights to the death, and rarely do the whales get wounded.

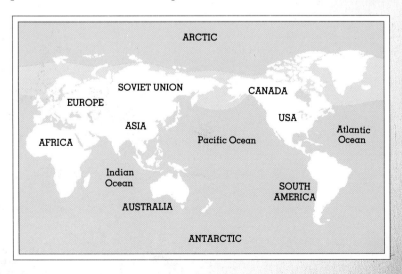

ARCTIC

SOVIET UNION

CANADA

EUROPE

USA

ASIA

Atlantic Ocean

AFRICA

Pacific Ocean

Indian Ocean

SOUTH AMERICA

AUSTRALIA

ANTARCTIC

SPERM WHALE
(Physeter macrocephalus)

The sperm whale is the largest of the toothed whales. A fully grown male may measure 66 feet (20 meters) from nose to tail and weigh about 55 tons. It is also the deepest diving whale, going down to depths of more than 6,600 feet (2,000 meters). It can stay down for more than an hour before having to surface for fresh air. When diving and surfacing, sperm whales move through the water at about 400 feet (130 meters) a minute.

To satisfy its huge appetite, a sperm whale feeds on large amounts of squid and fish, including sharks and rays. The stomach of one sperm whale contained 28,000 small squid!

In the darkness of deep water, the whale hunts mainly by sound not sight. It stays almost still, waiting in ambush for shoals of squid. Most of its prey measure less than 3 feet (1 meter) in length, but some are more than 50 feet (15 meters) long.

Occasionally, a sperm whale will swim along the sea bed, dropping its lower jaw to plough in the mud for all sorts of sea creatures to eat.

There she blows
Unlike most whales, the sperm whale has only one nostril, or blowhole, on the left side of its head. The spout of moist, used air shoots forward and outward from the blowhole or nostril.

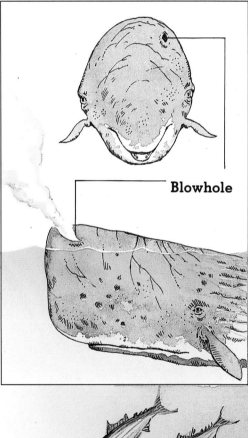

Blowhole

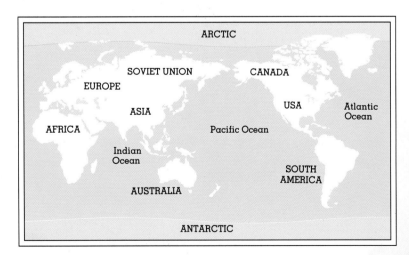

Around the world
Sperm whales are found from the Arctic to the Antarctic. In the fall, they swim toward warm tropical waters. In spring, they migrate toward the North and South Poles, where food supplies in summer will be plentiful.

Fight for supremacy
A sperm whale's head is often scarred by the sucker-marks of giant squid. The whale can gobble up small squid, but a large one will fight back. It wraps its tentacles around the whale's head and snaps at the whale with its beak. After a fierce struggle, the sperm whale usually succeeds in crushing the squid and swallowing it.

DOLPHINS AND PORPOISES

Dolphins are toothed whales with beak-like jaws, a pair of large V-shaped flippers, and usually a well-developed curved fin on the back. They feed mainly on fish, squid, and octopuses. There are 31 species of dolphin.

Porpoises are the smallest of the toothed whales, growing to about 5 feet (1.5 meters) in length. They have a rounded, beakless face with jaws armed with stubby or spade-like teeth. The fin on the back, if they have one, is small and triangular in shape. Porpoises feed primarily on fish. There are only six species.

Both dolphins and porpoises live close to land and this brings them in contact with people. Unfortunately, this results in many of them being killed for food, trapped in fishing nets, or poisoned by sea pollution. They are friendly animals, playing with swimmers and divers in shallow water and swimming alongside boats. They are also intelligent, having a language of whistles, chirps, clicks, and moans which they use to "talk" to one another and communicate with people.

A distinctive shape
It is easy to tell dolphins and porpoises apart as they have very different body shapes or outlines.

Dolphin

Porpoise

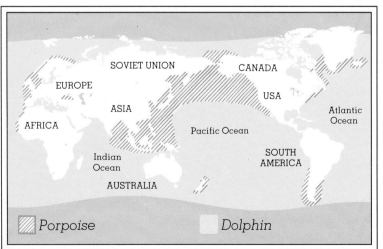

From the Atlantic to the Indian Ocean
Dolphins and porpoises are found almost worldwide, except in cold polar waters. Most species live in groups of up to 150.

12

Hunting in packs

Dolphins include the killer whale (Orcinus orca), the so-called wolf of the sea. It hunts and eats penguins, seals, rays, and even other dolphins. An adult killer whale, measuring up to 27 feet (8 meters) long, will chase and kill sharks. However, there are no reports of a killer whale harming a person.

RIVER DOLPHINS
(Family Platanistidae)

The Indus and Ganges river dolphins are almost blind, and the three other species of "freshwater dolphins" – from the Yangtze, Amazon, and La Plata – can see little better. They live most of the time in muddy estuaries where it is impossible to see things more than a few inches away. Eyesight is not important to these whales. They find their way around and capture food using echolocation.

River dolphins feed on fish and shellfish such as shrimps and lobsters. The La Plata river dolphin, which spends much of its time at sea, also eats squid and octopuses. The Ganges river dolphin is the largest species, growing to 8 1/2 feet (2.6 meters) from tip to tail and weighing up to 200 lb (90 kilograms). It also has the greatest lifespan – up to 28 years.

A loving embrace
Adult Ganges river dolphins are often seen in pairs. When they mate, the male and female rise up out of the water together, then they fall and roll over with a big splash.

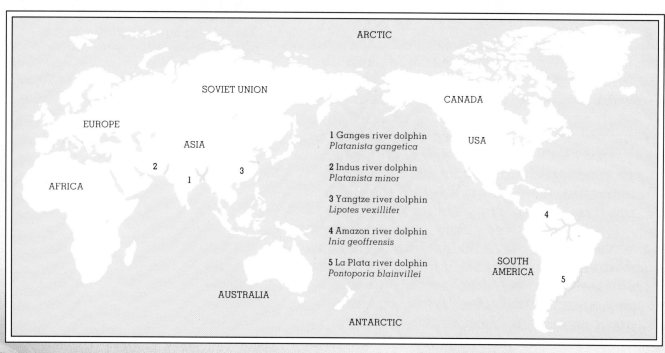

1 Ganges river dolphin
Platanista gangetica

2 Indus river dolphin
Platanista minor

3 Yangtze river dolphin
Lipotes vexillifer

4 Amazon river dolphin
Inia geoffrensis

5 La Plata river dolphin
Pontoporia blainvillei

A handful of species

There are five species of river dolphins. Each one is limited to a specific great river system of Asia or South America, from which they get their common name. In India river dolphins are named susa and in South America boutu.

Feeding on its back

The Amazon river dolphin has been known to swim upside-down, peering at the river bed in search of crabs and shrimps. The bristles on the top of its snout are very sensitive to touch and may be used to find food on the muddy bottom.

PORPOISES
(Family Phocoenidae)

The most familiar porpoise is the harbor porpoise (*Phocoena phocoena*). They travel in groups of five to 20 and are often seen around harbors and bays and swimming near ships. They can also be seen stranded on beaches.

Adult harbor porpoises mate when about 5 years old. The female is pregnant for 11 months. Mothers with their young often stay together in small groups. When the youngsters are about 8 months old, they start to feed for themselves.

The finless porpoise (*Neophocaena phocaenoides*) is so named because it does not have a fin on its back. Instead, there is a small dent where a fin would normally be and, behind this, a ridge of knobs or projections extending down to the tail. A baby finless porpoise rides on its mother's back clinging to these projections until it is able to swim fast.

Hanging on tight
The young have to hang on tight when a female finless porpoise comes up from a dive. She blows and swims fast along the water surface. Like all porpoises, when searching for fish, squid, and prawns to eat, she dives for up to 4 minutes, then surfaces and rolls over gently and slowly several times.

16

Moving in numbers

Harbor, or common, porpoises gather in groups of more than 100 when they migrate between cold Arctic and warm temperate waters. Porpoises rarely "porpoise" – leap through the air while swimming at speed. Only dolphins do this regularly.

BEAKED WHALES
(Family Ziphiidae)

Beaked whales are also known as the sword-nosed whales. Most have elongated jaws and all have a pair of grooves on the throat. They range in length from 13 to 40 feet (4 to 12 meters) and are found worldwide.

In species such as Shepherd's whale (*Tasmacetus shepherdi*), the beak is long and pointed and the jaws bear 40 or more teeth. In 12 of the 18 species of beaked whales, the beak is short and stubby and there is only one or two pairs of teeth in the lower jaw. Some have none at all.

Beaked whales feed mainly on squid and deep-sea fish. They also eat starfish and sea cucumbers, which live on and near the sea bed.

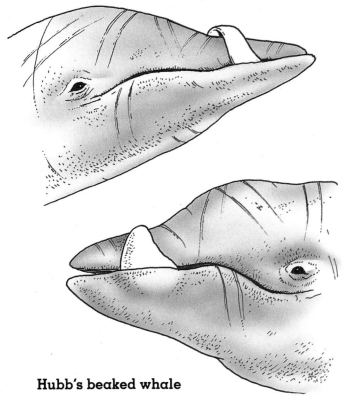

Strap-toothed whale

Hubb's beaked whale

Teeth patterns
Beaked whales with one or two pairs of teeth can be easily recognized by the position of the teeth. In the strap-toothed whale (Mesoplodon layardii), the teeth curve upward over the upper jaws. In Hubb's beaked whale (Mesoplodon carlhubbsi), each tooth in the pair is 7 inches (17 centimeters) high.

18

Battle scars
Adult male beaked whales often have scars on their backs from fights with others of the same species. The scars are teeth wounds made with slashes of the beak.

A wide but uncertain distribution
Beaked whales are found in all oceans, but as not many of them have been seen or their movements recorded, we are not certain of the range of most species.

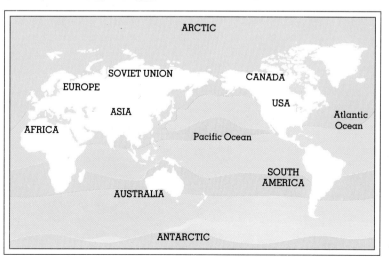

ARCTIC

SOVIET UNION

EUROPE

CANADA

ASIA

USA

Atlantic Ocean

AFRICA

Pacific Ocean

SOUTH AMERICA

AUSTRALIA

ANTARCTIC

BOTTLENOSE WHALES
(Hyperoodon ampullatus)

The northern bottlenose whale, a type of beaked whale, has a short beak with a big bulge above it. This led whalers to call it the barrel-head.

It is a big whale, growing up to 42 feet (12.8 meters) long and 9 tons in weight. It lives mainly in deep water, feeding on squid, its favorite food, and octopuses, lobsters, crabs, and fish.

Each year, the northern bottlenose or barrel-headed whale migrates with the changing seasons in the opposite direction from other whales. It is probably in search of rich supplies of squid. It spends the summer months in warm waters off the coasts of northwest North America and northeast Asia and around the islands of Japan. There, adults mate and pregnant females give birth. In the fall, adults and young swim north to Arctic waters.

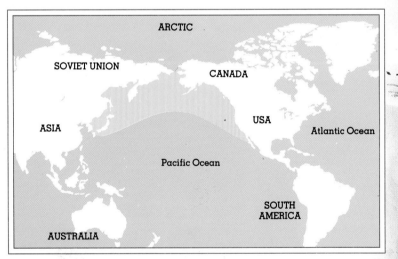

A northern whale
The northern bottlenose whale is found only in the North Pacific. There is a small population of a similar barrel-headed whale in the southern seas. This is regarded as a separate species, the southern bottlenose whale (Hyperoodon planifrons).

Hunted!

Up to 1972, when the hunting of bottlenose whales was stopped, more than 50,000 had been killed. In the early days of whaling, whales were killed with harpoons thrown by hand from small boats. Once explosive harpoon guns were introduced in the 1870s, the numbers of all whales killed increased greatly. Today, most whaling is banned.

BALEEN WHALES

There are 10 species of baleen whales and most of them survive largely on a diet of zooplankton – tiny animals living near the surface of the seas. The whales take large quantities of seawater into their mouths where bristles covering the baleen plates filter out the food. They scrape the food off the plates with their tongues and swallow it.

Baleen whales collect food in one of two ways: by skimming or by gulping. Skimmers such as the bowhead whale have huge scoop-like bottom jaws. The animals swim slowly along at the surface of the ocean with their mouths wide open. They constantly sieve zooplankton from the water.

"Rorquals," for example the sei and fin whales, and the other baleen species gulp at their food. *Rorqual* is taken from a mix of Scandinavian words describing the many pleats or grooves on the whales' throats. These expand each time the animals gulp a huge mouthful of water filled with small creatures. Then they contract, forcing the water over the baleen plates and out of the mouth. The food is trapped and then eaten.

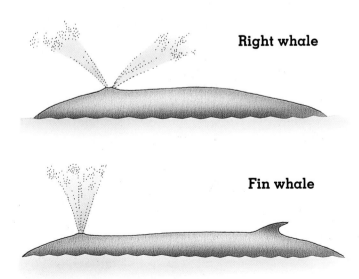

Right whale

Fin whale

Types of baleen
Baleen whales that feed by skimming have large, tall, triangular shaped heads with baleen plates up to 13 feet (4 meters) long. "Gulpers" have wider, flatter heads with shorter and wider plates. Their upper jaws fit into and between the lower ones.

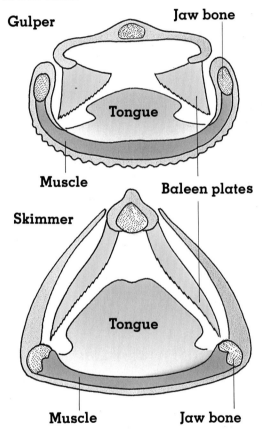

Spouts and fins
Whalers can readily distinguish some baleen whales by the shape of their spouts and fins. The right whale, for instance, has a double, V-shaped spout and no fin on its back. The fin whale has a single spout and a tall, curving fin set three-quarters of the way down its back.

Food scoops

The black right whale (Balaena glacialis) swims along at the surface of the sea. Its huge scoop-like jaws collect and filter krill (shrimp-like animals) from the water.

GRAY WHALE
(Eschrichtius robustus)

Every Christmas, thousands of Californians go to local beaches to watch small groups of gray whales as they migrate south. The whales are heading toward warm waters off Baja California, Mexico, where they will spend the winter months. They swim at speeds of about 5 miles an hour (8 km an hour), surfacing every 3 or 4 minutes to breathe.

In about March, gray whales head north to their summer feeding waters in the Arctic seas. They feed by gulping food as well as by scraping or sucking it from the mud on the sea floor. Often they swim on one side and plough along the bottom, filtering crabs, lobsters, mussels, and worms from the mud.

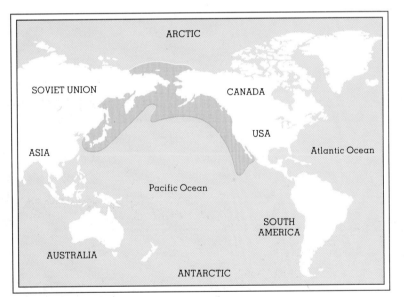

Champion migrants
There are two main populations of gray whales – eastern and western Pacific – each with its own migration route. The eastern population makes the longest migration of any mammal, 12,500 miles (20,400 kilometers), from the Arctic pack ice to Baja California and back. Little is known about the journeys of the western population.

24

Spy-hopping

When gray whales migrate, they can often be seen "spy-hopping." They stick their heads straight up out of the water to see the shore. This may be how they navigate, making sure they are on the correct migration route. When on the move, they swim in shallow water within about 1,000 yards (1 kilometer) of the shore. At other times they stay in deep water.

BLUE WHALE
(Balaenoptera musculus)

The largest of all animals feeds mainly on krill – shrimp-like animals only about 2 inches (5 centimeters) long. It swims through the vast swarms of krill that collect in surface waters, gulping in huge mouthfuls. A blue whale may eat 4 tons of food a day – that is at least 4 million krill. On this diet, adult blue whales grow to over 89 feet (27 meters) in length and weigh up to 150 tons – more than the weight of 25 full-grown elephants.

Blue whales are ready to mate when they are about 5 years old. Mating takes place in warm waters in summer, and the females each give birth to a single calf about 11 months later. By 7 months of age the youngster has started to feed for itself. The mother does not mate while she is caring for her calf, so she breeds only once every 2 or 3 years. Blue whales have a lifespan of up to 80 years.

Thirsty work

At birth a blue whale is about 23 feet (7 meters) long and weighs 2.5 tons. It grows fast on the milk it gets from its mother, doubling its size in 6 or 7 months. It drinks up to 160 gallons (600 liters) of her milk every day.

Smaller southern relatives

There are only about 12,000 blue whales in the world. They are found in all seas, but three main populations are recognized – north Pacific, north Atlantic, and the southern hemisphere. In the southern Indian Ocean so-called pygmy blue whales are found. They are about three-quarters of the size of the normal ones.

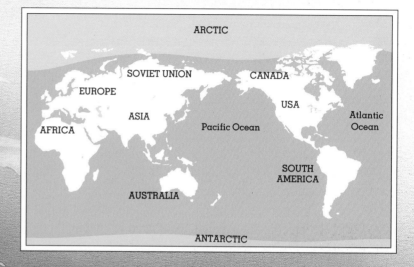

HUMPBACK WHALE
(Megaptera novaeangliae)

"Singer of the seas" might be a more suitable name for this large whale, which weighs up to 65 tons. Like a songbird, it constantly sings a melody. It is called "humpback" because it arches its back out of the water as it dives.

The humpback's song includes sounds that have been described as groans, whos, yups, chirps, and oos. The sounds can be heard above and under water over distances of 115 miles (185 kilometers). Family groups of three or four whales use these sounds to keep in contact. Females also use them to tell males that they are ready to mate.

Humpback whales feed on krill and fish. They trap shoals of fish by creating "bubble nets." They set up a curtain of bubbles by forcing air out through their blowholes as they swim upward in a spiral from a depth of about 50 feet (15 meters). The fish are confused and stay together within the net. Then the whales surface open-mouthed and gulp them in.

Knucklehead
This English name for the humpback whale refers to the knobs and bumps on its head and flippers. These are often covered in barnacles like those found on the bottoms of boats. The barnacles do not harm the whales.

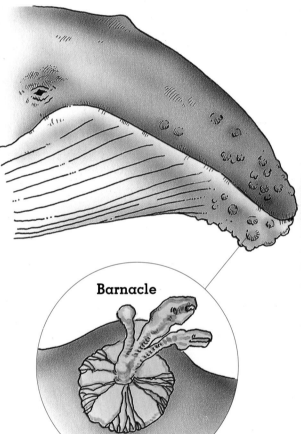

Barnacle

Found in all oceans
Humpbacks are found in all oceans. They spend most of their time in deep water. However, during their yearly migrations from Arctic and Antarctic feeding grounds to breeding areas in warm tropical waters, they swim close to the shore.

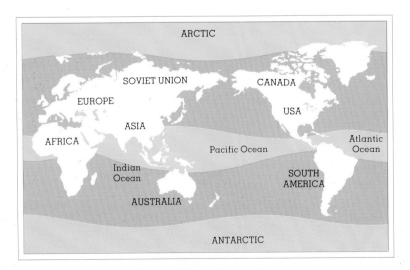

Frolics and acrobatics
Humpbacks are joyful animals. Although large (up to 50 feet (15 meters) long), they hurl themselves out of the water in courtship displays or just for fun. As well as arching their backs, they fling their tails in the air before diving, and occasionally slap the water with their huge wing-like flippers to make a sound like a rifle shot.

MINKE WHALE
(Balaenoptera acutorostrata)

In the southern oceans, close to the continent of Antarctica, minke whales often swim among the pack ice in search of krill, squid, and fish. Sometimes they get trapped in pools in the ice as the seas freeze over. Unless the whales can surface to breathe, they will die.

The minke whale lives mainly in groups of up to 10 in cool or cold waters. It can swim at speeds of about 19 miles an hour (30 km an hour). It will swim alongside a moving ship, dive down beneath the hull, and surface on the other side.

A natural submarine
Seen head-on, the minke whale looks like a nuclear submarine with fins. There is a distinct ridge along the top of its head. It is also known as the piked whale because of its sharply pointed head and the prominent fin on its back.

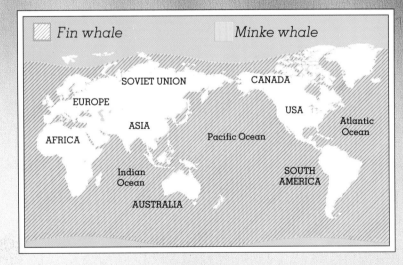

Fin whale   Minke whale

SOVIET UNION   CANADA
EUROPE
USA
ASIA
Atlantic
Ocean
Pacific Ocean
AFRICA
Indian
Ocean
SOUTH
AMERICA
AUSTRALIA

In the warm shallows
Minke whales are found worldwide. Pregnant females, and mothers and their young, tend to stay in warmer waters, often swimming into estuaries.

The commonest baleen whale
The fin whale ranges from polar to tropical waters. Unlike most other whales, individuals regularly cross the equator between the northern and southern hemispheres, and some have even been found in the Mediterranean Sea.

FIN WHALE
(Balaenoptera physalus)

The fin whale, which at about 70 tons and up to 82 feet (25 meters) in length is the second largest species, is an especially friendly giant. It will allow a small boat to come close enough for people to touch its back. It is also a powerful swimmer, reaching speeds of up to 25 miles an hour (40 km an hour). It dives to depths of 1,000 feet (300 meters) and can stay down for almost half an hour.

This rorqual feeds on a wide variety of animals ranging from krill and squid to fish such as sardine, anchovy, and capelin. Its throat has up to 100 deep pleats, which can open out to form an enormous sac.

A tasty side-dish
Whenever the fin whale finds a particularly large shoal of small fish or swarm of krill near the surface, it rolls on to its right side with its left flipper in the air. Then, with its mouth wide open, it makes a sideways scoop at the food.

BRYDE'S WHALE
(Balaenoptera edeni)

This whale is most common in the warm waters off southern Africa, where it hunts for food among the huge shoals of fish such as pilchard. Its common name is taken from J. Bryde, a Norwegian ambassador to South Africa, who built a whaling factory there at the beginning of the twentieth century.

Bryde's whale is similar to the sei whale although it is usually smaller. The male grows up to 43 feet (13 meters) in length compared to about 57 feet (17 meters) in the sei whale. Females tend to be 3 feet (a meter) or so larger. Both sexes are ready to mate when they are about 7 years old.

Beached!
Bryde's whales swim close to the shore. Sometimes they get stranded on beaches and die.

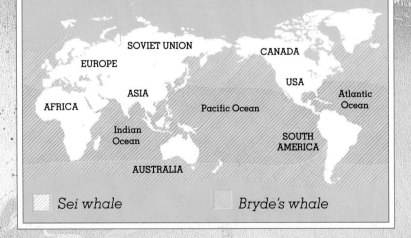

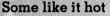

Some like it hot
Bryde's whale spends most of its time in tropical and sub-tropical waters. There are several distinct populations.

SOVIET UNION

CANADA

EUROPE

USA

ASIA

Pacific Ocean

Atlantic Ocean

AFRICA

Indian Ocean

SOUTH AMERICA

AUSTRALIA

Sei whale

Bryde's whale

Migrating in small groups
In late summer, sei whales journey in groups of up to five from cool polar to warm temperate or tropical waters. In spring, they make the return trip.

SEI WHALE
(Balaenoptera borealis)

The sei whale is probably the fastest swimmer of the large whales – up to 30 miles an hour (50 km an hour). Before engine-powered boats, its speed was the secret of its survival as it could outswim whaling ships.

This species feeds on krill and other small crustaceans, skimming at the surface to eat. An adult eats about 1 ton of food a day. Unlike Bryde's whale, it dives gently and quietly, and it often lies still at the surface for several minutes. In the fall sei whales migrate from cool polar waters to warm tropical waters, returning the following spring.

Different heads
The sei and Bryde's whale are very similar. One way to tell them apart is from the ridges on the tops of their heads. Bryde's whale has three ridges, the sei whale has only one.

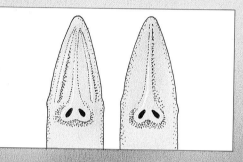

RIGHT WHALES
(Balaena species)

There are three species of "right" whales, so-called because they were the right whales to hunt from the old-time open-boat whalers. Compared to other whales, they are slow-moving, they float when killed, and they have lots of valuable body oils and baleen. Also, they swim close to the shore.

The black right whale is the most widespread. It grows to 60 feet (18 meters) in length. Its most characteristic feature is a series of growths on top of its head, the largest of which is called the bonnet. Like all right whales, it feeds on plankton by skimming.

The Greenland right whale grows to 66 feet (20 meters) in length. In contrast to the black right whale, it lacks any lumps on its head. Its skull is distinctly bow shaped, hence its other name of bowhead whale.

The pygmy right whale reaches only 16 feet (5 meters) from tip to tail. It is quite rare and little is known about its habits and way of life.

Black right whale (*Balaena glacialis*)

Rock garden
The lumps on the head of a black right whale are covered with barnacles. Many parasitic worms and lice also live on the whale. The pattern of colonies of these "hangers-on" is different for each individual, helping scientists to recognize them.

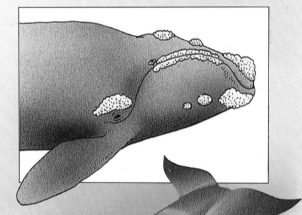

Greenland right whale
(*Balaena mysticetus*)

Pygmy right whale
(*Balaena marginata*)

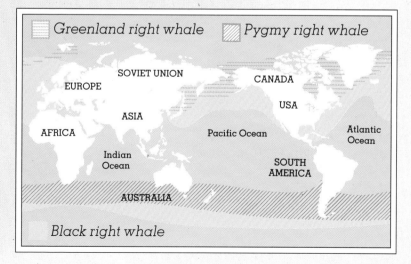

▤ Greenland right whale   ▨ Pygmy right whale

SOVIET UNION   CANADA

EUROPE

USA

ASIA

AFRICA

Pacific Ocean

Atlantic
Ocean

Indian
Ocean

SOUTH
AMERICA

AUSTRALIA

Black right whale

Separate ranges
*The black right whale is distributed
throughout temperate and cool seas.
The Greenland right whale lives in
Arctic waters. The pygmy right whale
ranges throughout cool southern seas.*

WHALES UNDER THREAT

People have hunted whales for more than 1,000 years. Whale meat, especially from baleen whales, is still eaten by some people and is also used to make pet foods. Blubber (the thick layer of fat whales develop to keep themselves warm in the water) is a source of oil that can be used as a fuel. Other whale products have been used to make margarines, soaps, fertilizers, smokeless candles, and lubricating oils for machines. Whalebone (baleen) was at one time used as stiffeners in ladies' corsets and shirt collars.

Modern whaling started in about 1860, when fast catcher boats and explosive harpoon guns were developed. Each year, tens of thousands of whales, in particular species such as the blue, sperm, and black right, were killed. Their populations had no time to recover so that by the beginning of the twentieth century, many whales were threatened with extinction. In the 1930s, the major whaling nations – Japan, Iceland, Norway, Canada, the Soviet Union, and Britain – agreed to hunt only selected species.

Today, commercial whaling is banned, although some does go on, supposedly for "scientific purposes," to find out more about the animals' way of life. People whose lives have for centuries depended on whales, for example the Inuit of North America and islanders of the Faroes in the North Atlantic, still kill whales for their meat and oil. But they take only a few hundred whales each year, and the whales can breed quickly enough to maintain their numbers.

The greatest threat to whales now is probably pollution of the oceans. This kills many types of creatures in the sea, directly or indirectly through food chains – if krill and fish die, the whales that feed on them will also die.

Whaling ships
Modern whaling ships were used like factories at sea. Whales were hauled on board, their bodies were cut up and the various parts were processed.

INDEX